The World Waits

Inspired by
"The Godhead here in hiding, whom I do adore,
masked by these bare shadows, shape and nothing more." *

*Thomas Aquinas as translated by Gerard Manley Hopkins

SOPHIA
INSTITUTE PRESS

Text copyright © 2023 Elizabeth Pham
Art copyright © 2023 Jen Olson

Printed in the United States of America.

Sophia Institute Press®
Box 5284, Manchester, NH 03108
1-800-888-9344
www.SophiaInstitute.com

Sophia Institute Press® is a registered trademark of Sophia Institute.

ISBN: 978-1-64413-796-3
LCCN: 2023940265

2nd printing

The World Waits

Elizabeth Pham

Illustrated by Jen Olson

SOPHIA INSTITUTE PRESS
Manchester, NH

The world is waiting.

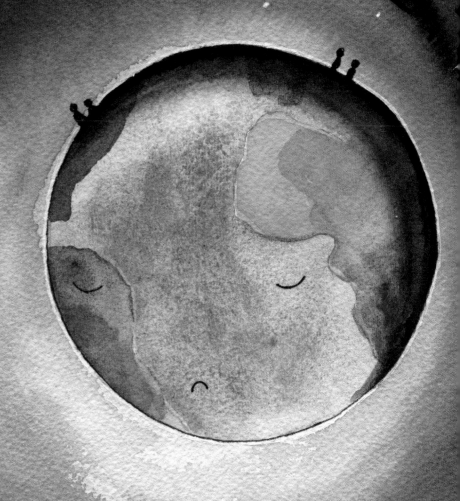

Sometimes, it gets
tired of waiting.

Sometimes, it feels cold...

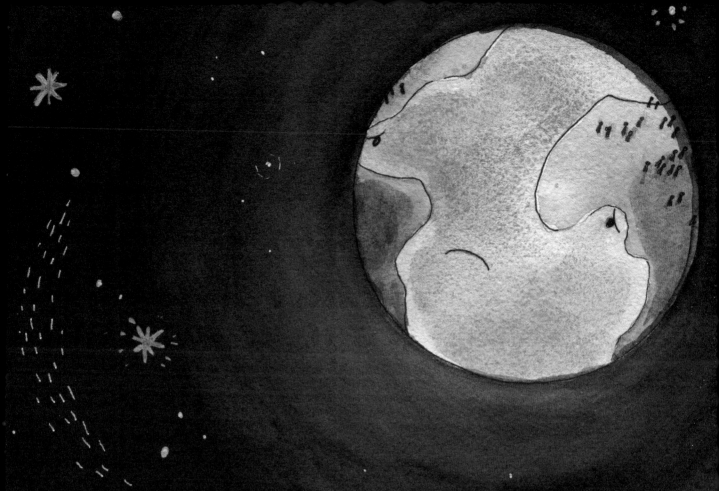

and tired...

and sad.

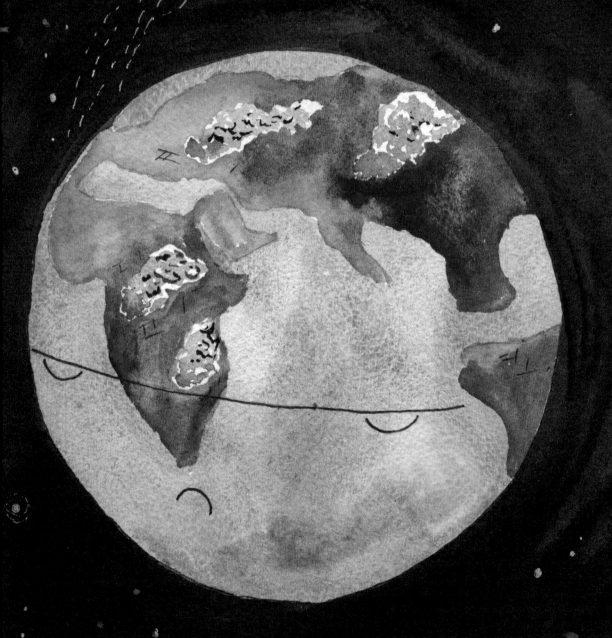

It is a long, long wait.

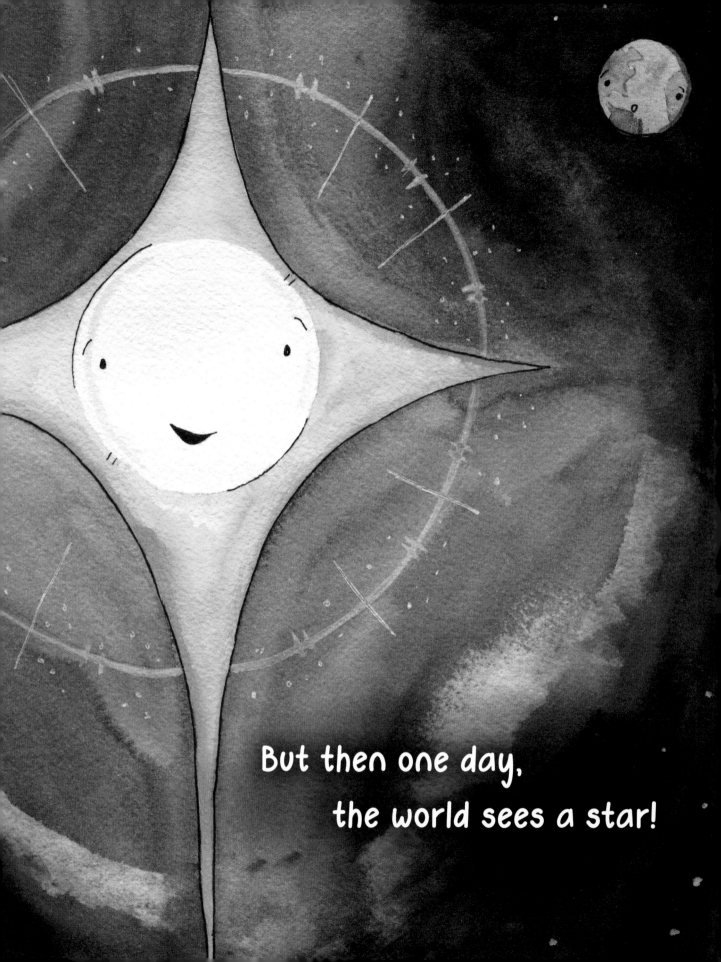

But then one day,
the world sees a star!

The star sees the world.

Suddenly, the world feels warm...

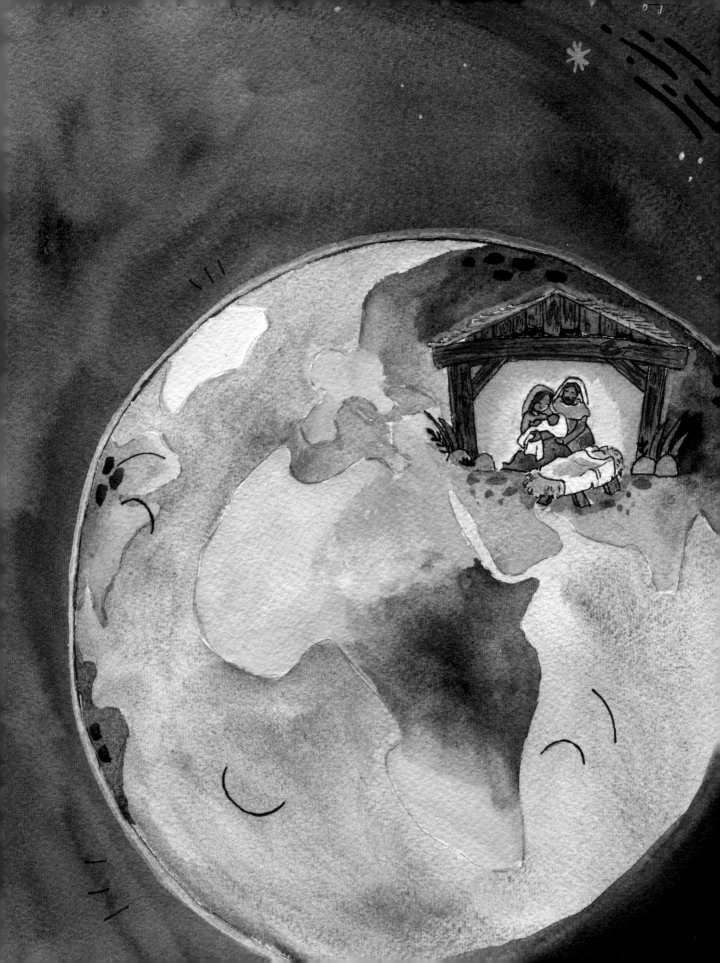

and hopeful...

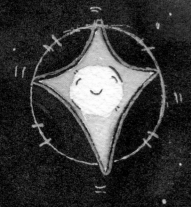

and filled with
tidings of great joy!

The star left,
almost as quickly as it came.

The world did not understand...

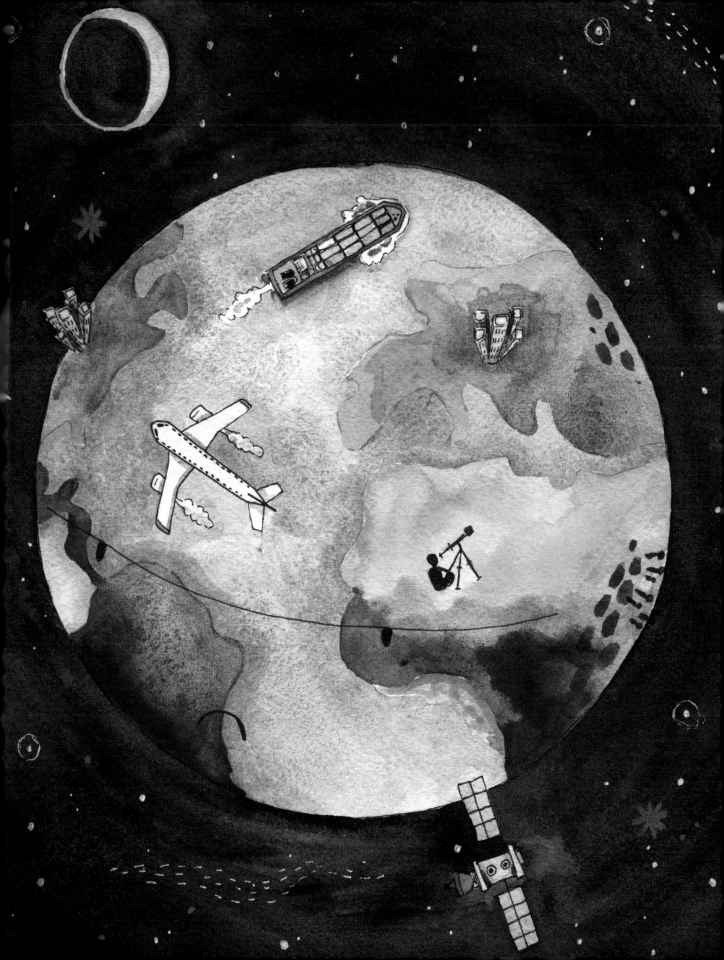

but neither did the world forget.

every moment...

the world waits.

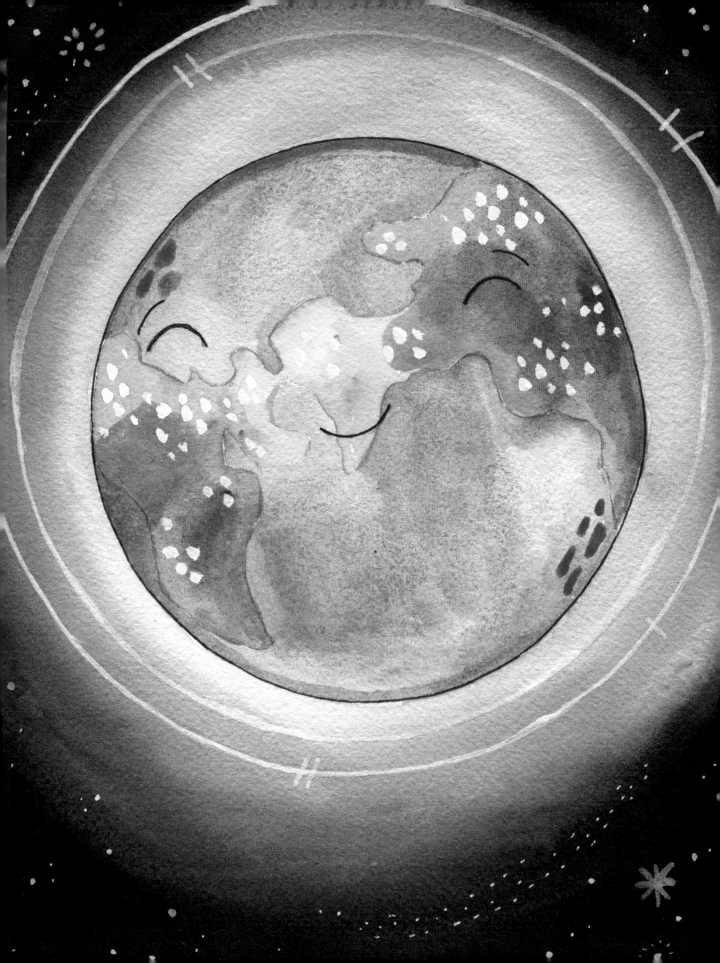